PIANO • VOCAL • GUITAR

highlights of the 20's & 30's

20's

1921
1922
1923 1924 1925
1926 1927
1928
1929

&

30's

ISBN 1-56922-018-2

CREATIVE CONCEPTS
P U B L I S H I N G

EXCLUSIVELY DISTRIBUTED BY

HAL•LEONARD®
CORPORATION
7777 W. BLUEMOUND RD. P.O. BOX 13819 MILWAUKEE, WI 53213

Visit Hal Leonard Online at
www.halleonard.com

Table of Contents

AIN'T MISBEHAVIN'
from AIN'T MISBEHAVIN'

Words by ANDY RAZAF
Music by THOMAS "FATS" WALLER and HARRY BROOKS

1. No one to talk with, all by my-self, no one to walk with,_ but I'm
2.,3. *(See additional lyrics)*

hap-py on a shelf. Ain't mis-be-hav-in', sav-in' my love for

you. you.

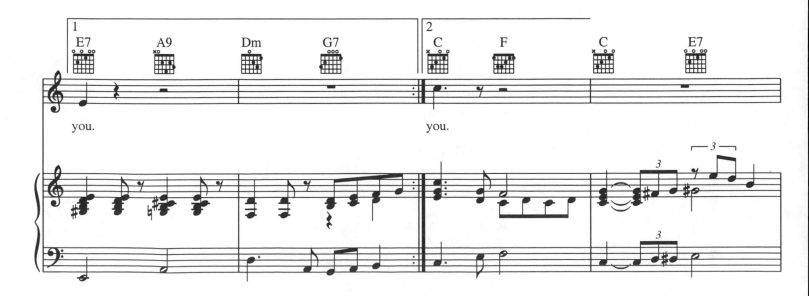

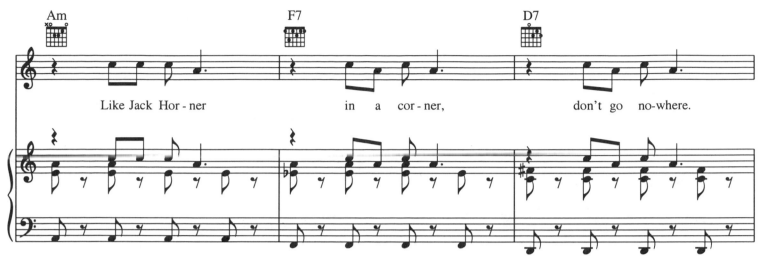

Like Jack Hor-ner in a cor-ner, don't go no-where.

Why do I care ___ Your kiss-es are ___ worth wait-ing for. ___

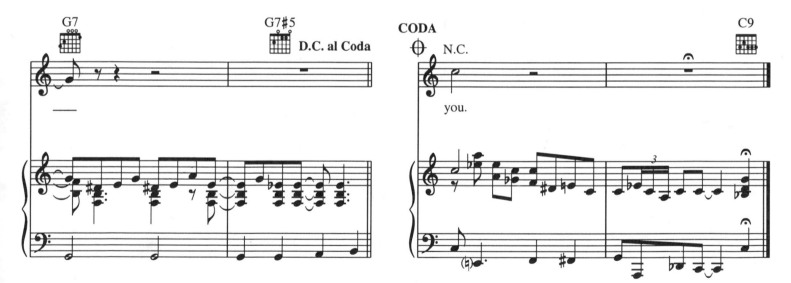

D.C. al Coda

CODA

you.

Additional Lyrics

2. Now I know for certain you're the one I love.
I'm through with flirtin', just you I'm dreamin' of.
Ain't misbehavin', savin' my love for you. *(To Bridge)*

3. I don't stay out late; I don't care to go.
I'm home about eight, just me and my radio.
Ain't misbehavin', savin' my love for you.

APRIL IN PARIS

Words by E.Y. HARBURG
Music by VERNON DUKE

APRIL SHOWERS
from BOMBO

Words by B.G. DeSYLVA
Music by LOUIS SILVERS

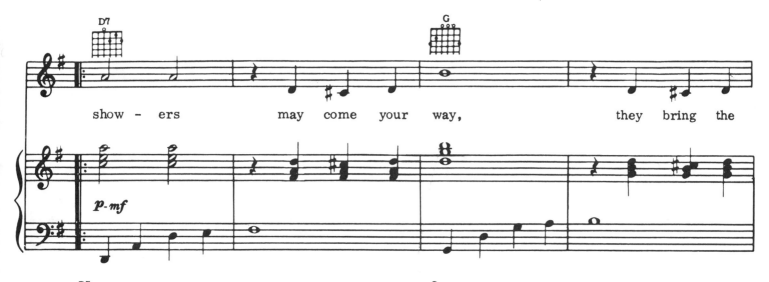

show - ers may come your way, they bring the

flow - ers that bloom in May; so if it's

rain - ing, _____ have no re - grets _____ be - cause it

is - n't rain - ing rain you know, it's rain - ing vi - o - lets And where you

BABY FACE

Words and Music by BENNY DAVIS
and HARRY AKST

15

THE BEST THINGS IN LIFE ARE FREE
from GOOD NEWS!

Music and Lyrics by B.G. DeSYLVA,
LEW BROWN and RAY HENDERSON

THE BIRTH OF THE BLUES
from GEORGE WHITE'S SCANDALS OF 1926

Words by B.G. DeSYLVA and LEW BROWN
Music by RAY HENDERSON

BREEZIN' ALONG WITH THE BREEZE

Words by HAVEN GILLESPIE and SEYMOUR SIMONS
Music by RICHARD A. WHITING

24

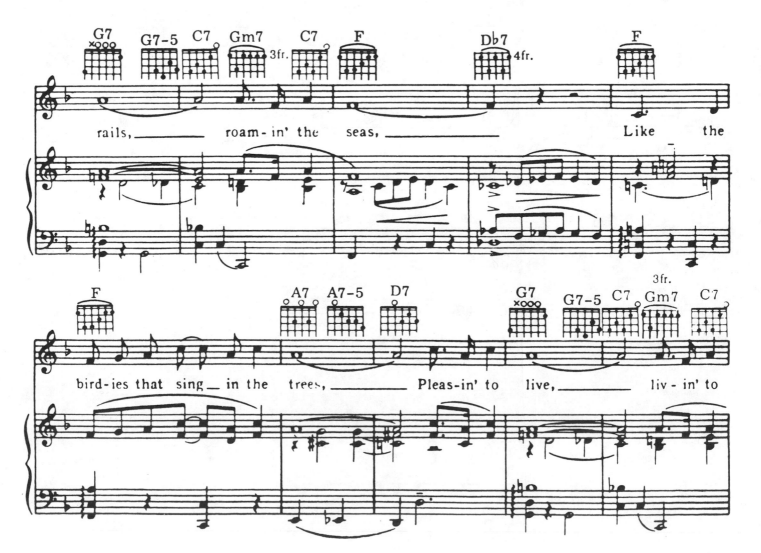

CALIFORNIA, HERE I COME

Words and Music by AL JOLSON,
B.G. DeSYLVA and JOSEPH MEYER

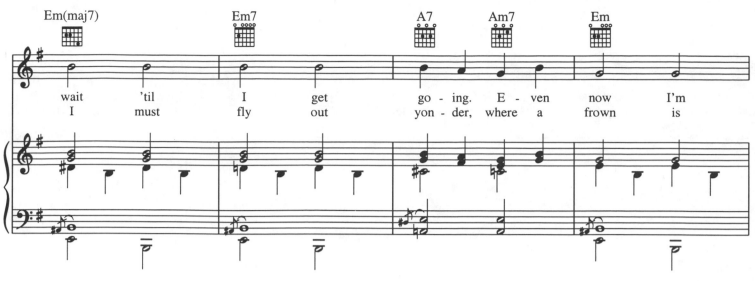

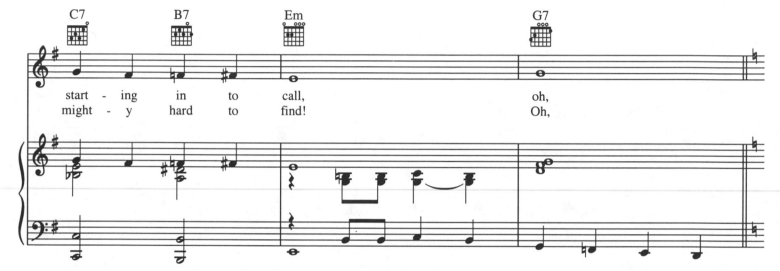

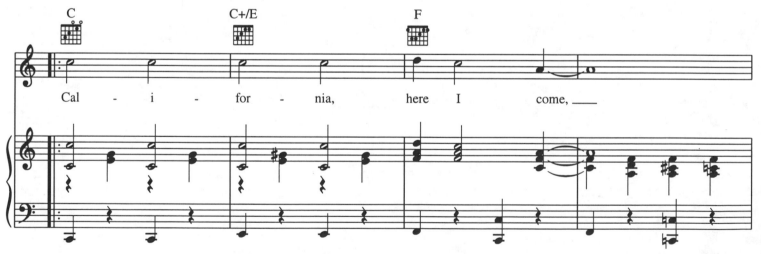

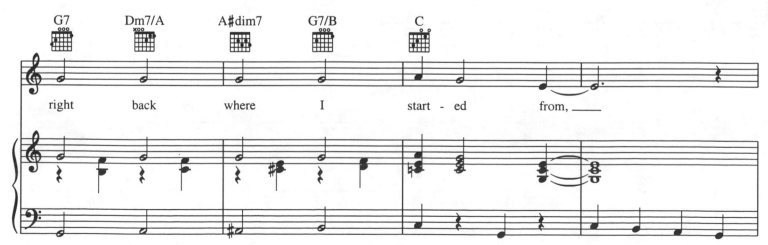

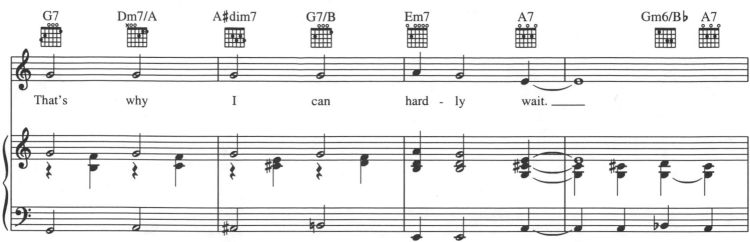

That's why I can hard - ly wait. ____

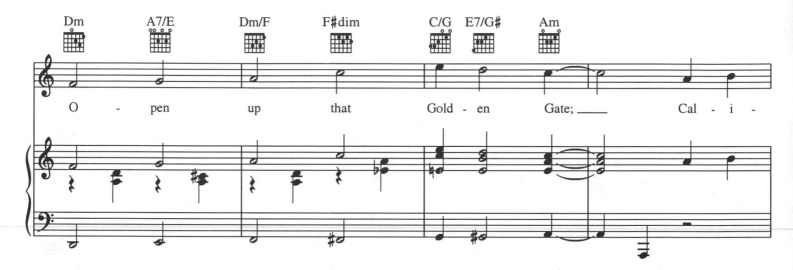

O - pen up that Gold - en Gate; ____ Cal - i -

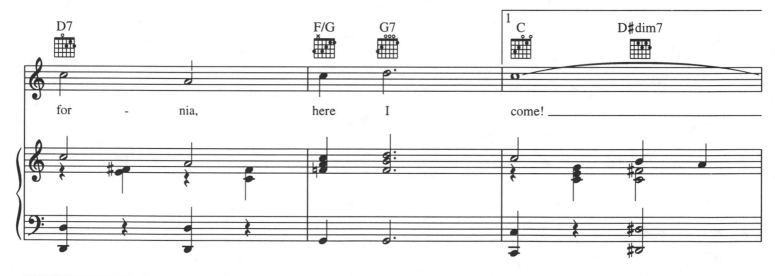

for - nia, here I come! ____

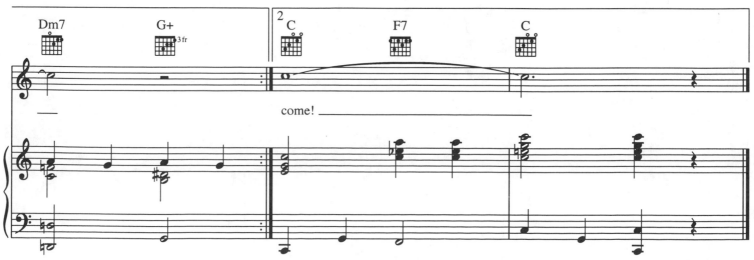

____ come! ____

DARN THAT DREAM

Lyric by EDDIE DE LANGE
Music by JIMMY VAN HEUSEN

Slowly

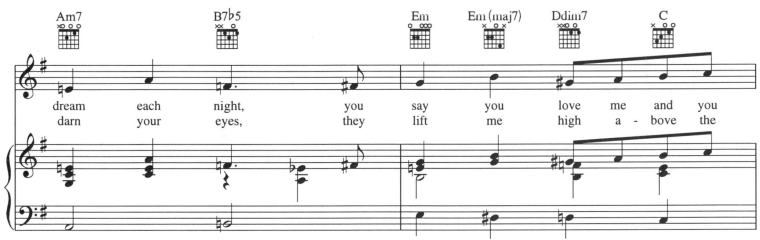

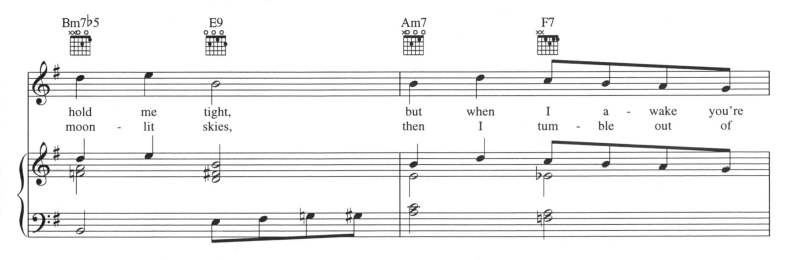

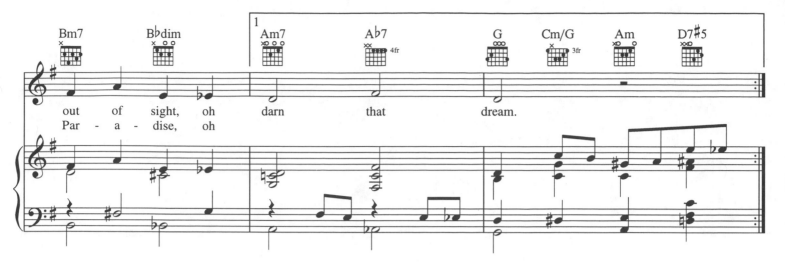

out of sight, oh darn that dream.
Par - a - dise, oh

darn that dream. Darn that one track

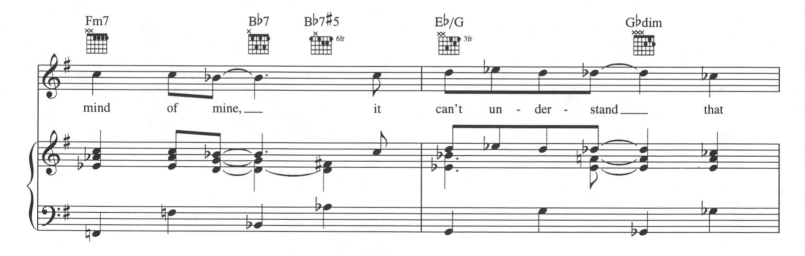

mind of mine, ___ it can't un - der - stand ___ that

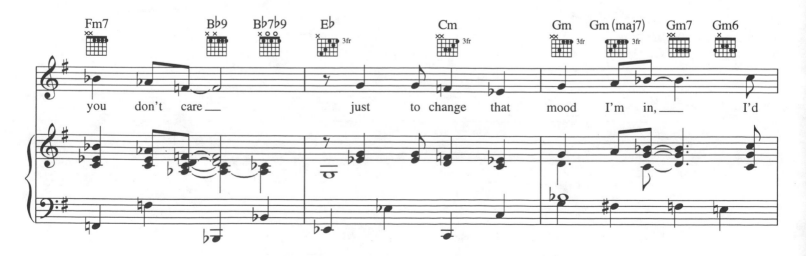

you don't care ___ just to change that mood I'm in, ___ I'd

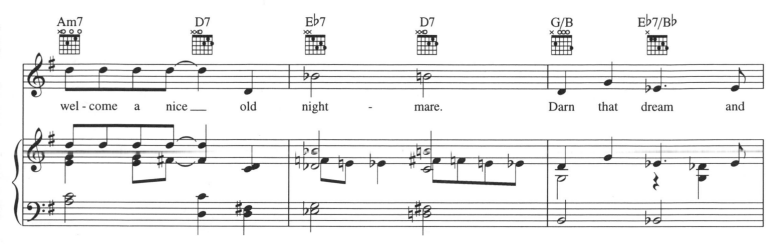

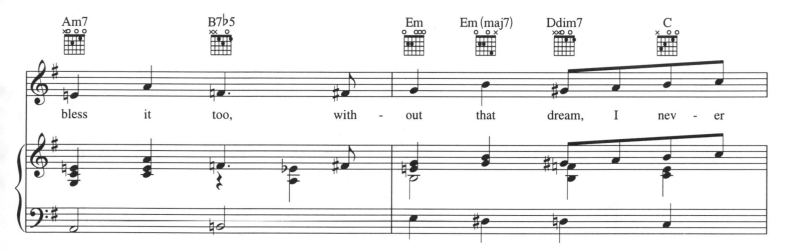

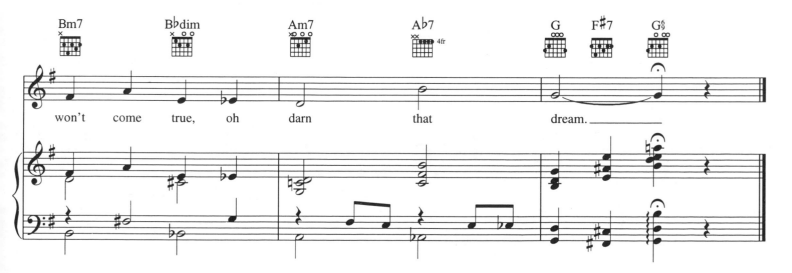

DO IT AGAIN

Words by B.G. DeSYLVA
Music by GEORGE GERSHWIN

Tell me, tell me, what did you do to me? I just got a

thrill that was new to me, when your two lips were

pressed to mine. When you held me,

DREAM A LITTLE DREAM OF ME

Words by GUS KAHN
Music by WILBUR SCHWANDT
and FABIAN ANDREE

EAST OF THE SUN
(And West of the Moon)

Words and Music by
BROOKS BOWMAN

Slowly, with expression

East of the sun _____ and west of the moon, _____

we'll build a dream - house _____ of love, dear. Near to the sun in the

A GOOD MAN IS HARD TO FIND

Words and Music by
EDDIE GREEN

44

FIND OUT WHAT THEY LIKE AND HOW THEY LIKE IT

Words by ANDY RAZAF
Music by THOMAS "FATS" WALLER

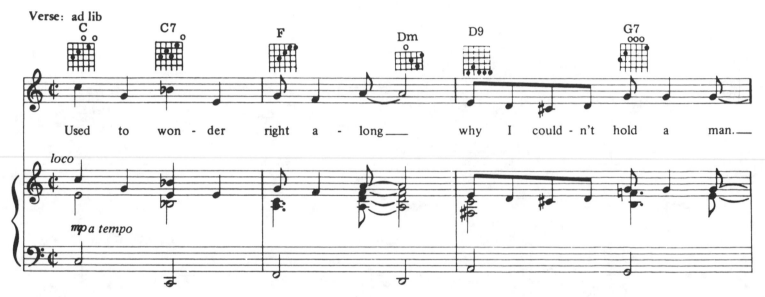

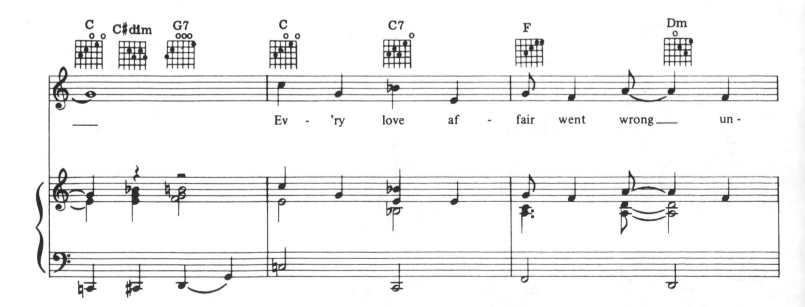

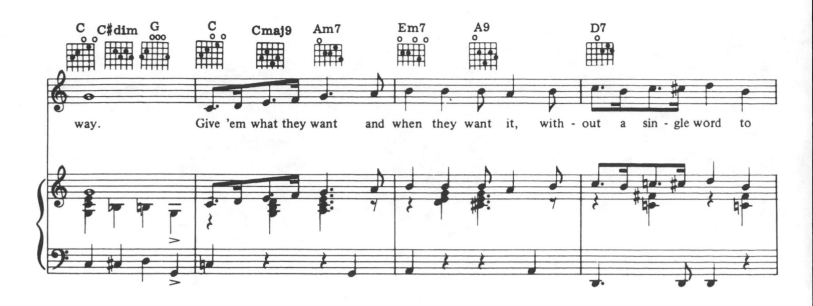

way.
Give 'em what they want and when they want it, with - out a sin - gle word to

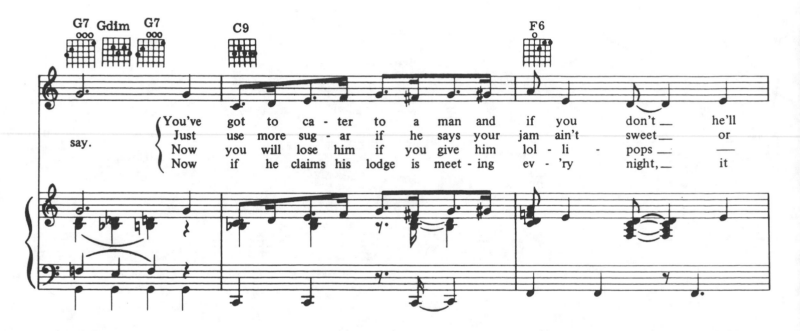

say.
You've got to ca - ter to a man and if you don't __ he'll
Just use more sug - ar if he says your jam ain't sweet __ or __
Now you will lose him if you give him lol - li - pops __ — __
Now if he claims his lodge is meet - ing ev - 'ry night, __ it

find some oth - er gal to do the things you won't. __
he will sneak for his des - sert a - cross the street. __
when you know he's cra - zy just to have some chops. __
means you do not han - dle all your busi - ness right. __

Find out what they like, and

GUILTY

Words and Music by GUS KAHN,
HARRY AKST and RICHARD A. WHITING

51

HAVE YOU EVER BEEN LONELY?
(Have You Ever Been Blue?)

Words by GEORGE BROWN
Music by PETER DeROSE

8va- - - ⌐

I AIN'T GOT NOBODY
(And Nobody Cares for Me)

Words by ROGER GRAHAM
Music by SPENCER WILLIAMS
and DAVE PEYTON

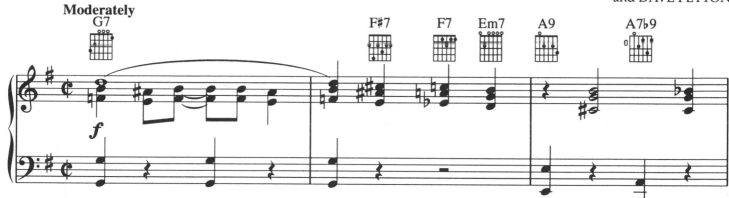

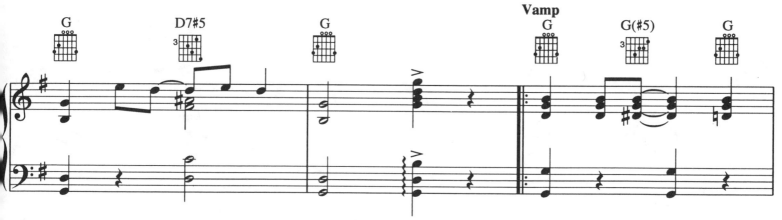

There's a say - ing go - ing 'round, _ And
Won't some - bod - y go and find, _ My

HONEYSUCKLE ROSE
from AIN'T MISBEHAVIN'

Words by ANDY RAZAF
Music by THOMAS "FATS" WALLER

Have no use for oth- er sweets of an- y kind, since the day you came a-

round. From the start, I in- stant- ly made up my mind,

I CAN'T GIVE YOU ANYTHING BUT LOVE

from BLACKBIRDS OF 1928

By JIMMY McHUGH
and DOROTHY FIELDS

Moderately

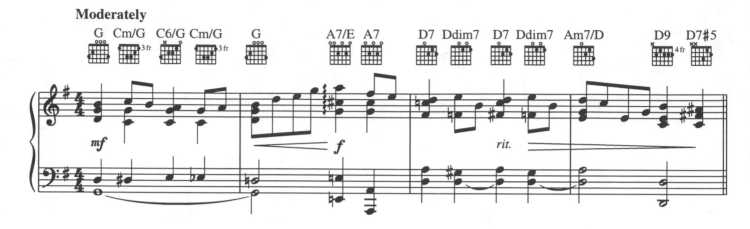

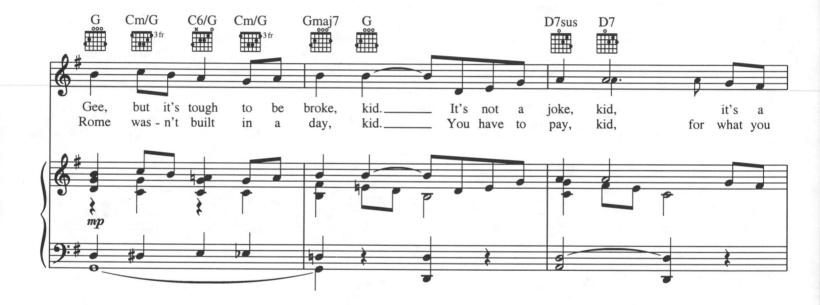

Gee, but it's tough to be broke, kid.___ It's not a joke, kid, it's a
Rome was-n't built in a day, kid.___ You have to pay, kid, for what you

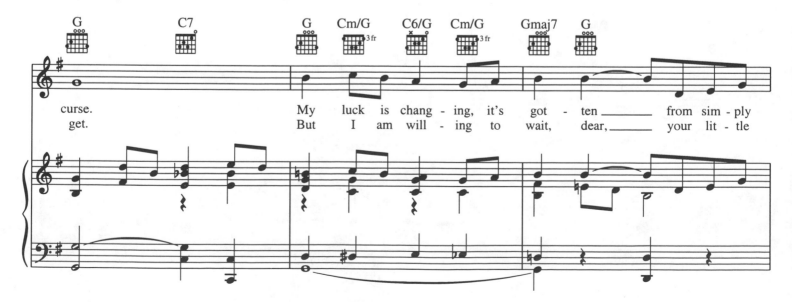

curse. My luck is chang-ing, it's got-ten ___ from sim-ply
get. But I am will-ing to wait, dear, ___ your lit-tle

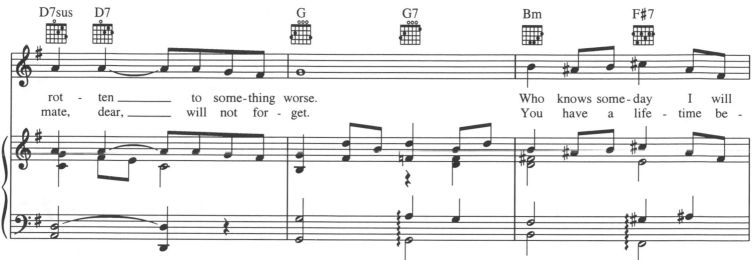

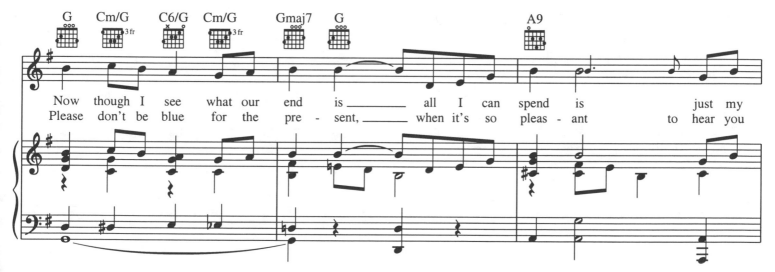

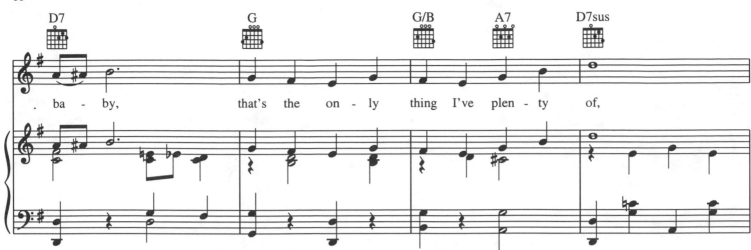

ba - by, that's the on - ly thing I've plen - ty of,

ba - by. Dream a - while, scheme a - while, we're sure to find, —

— hap - pi - ness and I guess all those things you've

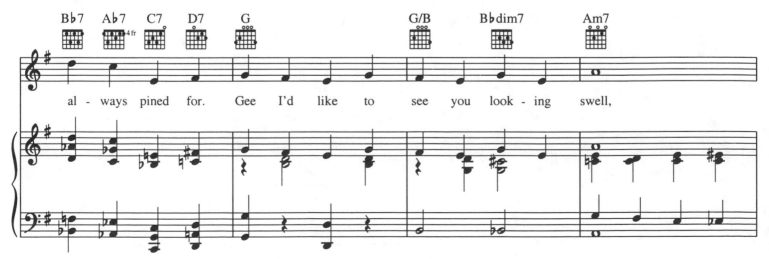

al - ways pined for. Gee I'd like to see you look - ing swell,

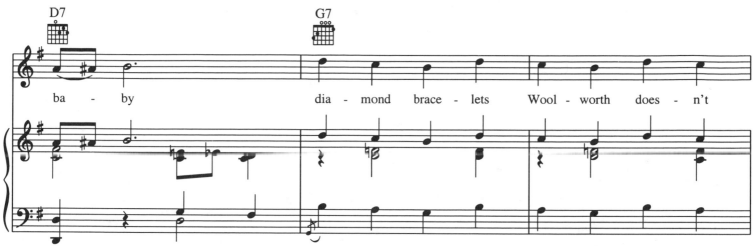

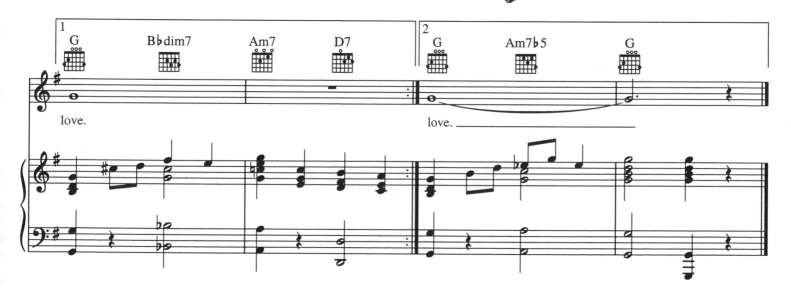

I DON'T KNOW WHY
(I Just Do)

Lyric by ROY TURK
Music by FRED E. AHLERT

Slowly, with feeling

do. I Don't Know Why____ you thrill me like you do.____

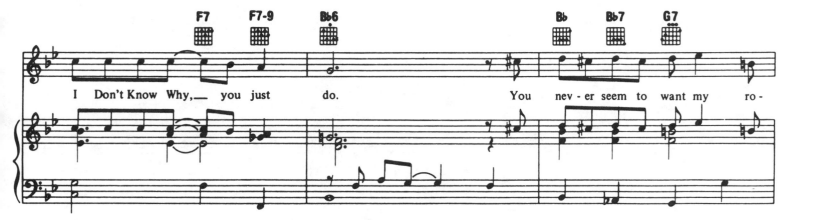

I Don't Know Why,____ you just do. You nev - er seem to want my ro -

manc - ing, the on - ly time you hold me is when we're danc - ing,

I Don't Know Why____ I love you like I do,____ I Don't Know Why,____ I just do.

I FOUND A MILLION DOLLAR BABY

(In a Five and Ten Cent Store)
from FUNNY LADY

Lyric by BILLY ROSE
and MORT DIXON
Music by HARRY WARREN

Love comes a-long like a pop-u-lar song, An-y-time or an-y-where at all.

Love used to be quite a stran-ger to me Did-n't know a sen-ti-men-tal word,

Rain or sun-shine, spring or fall,

Thoughts of kiss-ing seemed ab-surd.

Five And Ten Cent Store; The rain con-tin-ued for an hour, — I hung a-round for three or four, A-round a mil-lion dol-lar ba-by In a Five and Ten Cent Store. She was sell-ing chi - na And when she made those

I LIKE THE LIKES OF YOU

Words by E.Y. HARBURG
Music by VERNON DUKE

Lad - y, last Sat - ur - day, Or was it yes - ter - day?

I was re - hears - ing a speech. Real - ly I think_ it's a

I THOUGHT ABOUT YOU

Words by JOHNNY MERCER
Music by JIMMY VAN HEUSEN

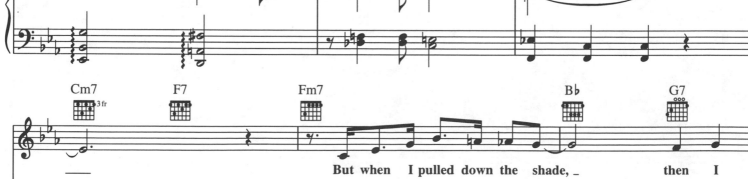

I'LL BUILD A STAIRWAY TO PARADISE

from GEORGE WHITE'S SCANDALS

Words by B.G. DeSYLVA and IRA GERSHWIN
Music by GEORGE GERSHWIN

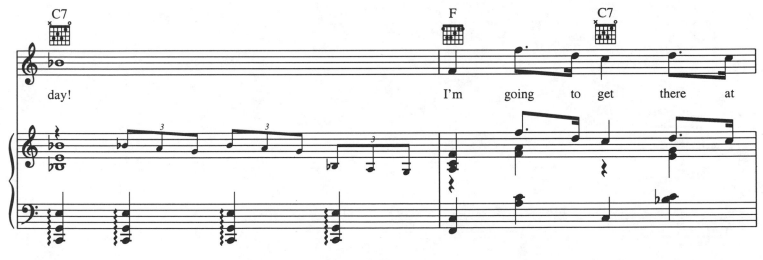

I'M GONNA SIT RIGHT DOWN AND WRITE MYSELF A LETTER

from AIN'T MISBEHAVIN'

Lyric by JOE YOUNG
Music by FRED E. AHLERT

I'VE GOT THE WORLD ON A STRING

Lyric by TED KOEHLER
Music by HAROLD ARLEN

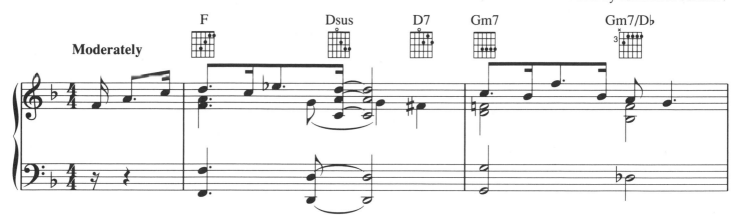

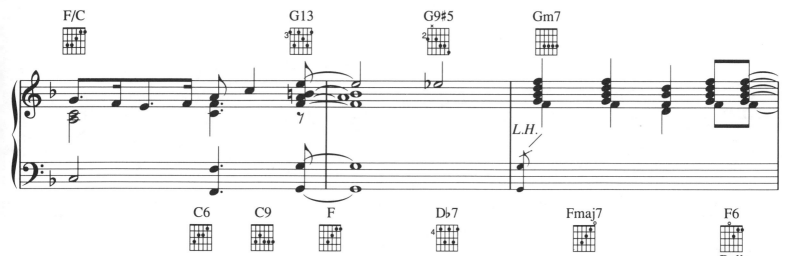

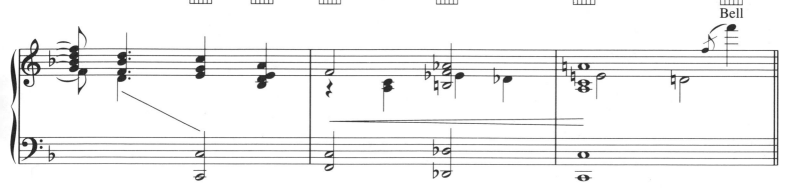

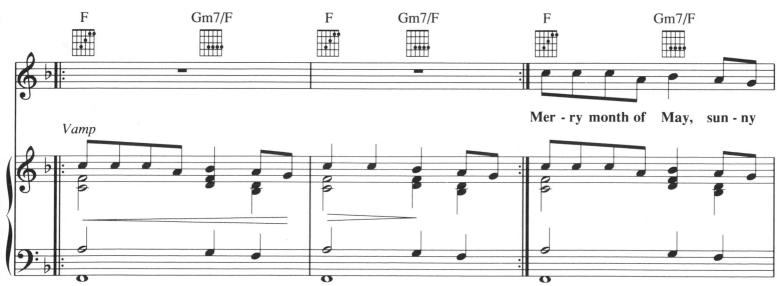

Mer - ry month of May, sun - ny

IF YOU KNEW SUSIE
(Like I Know Susie)

Words and Music by B.G. DeSYLVA
and JOSEPH MEYER

IN THE MOOD

By JOE GARLAND

Swinging

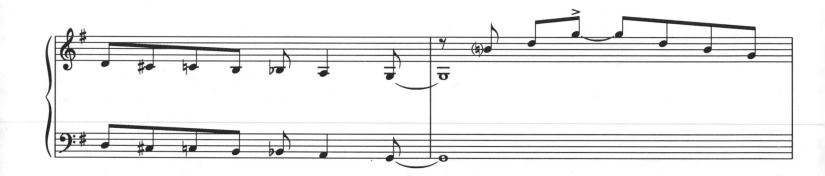

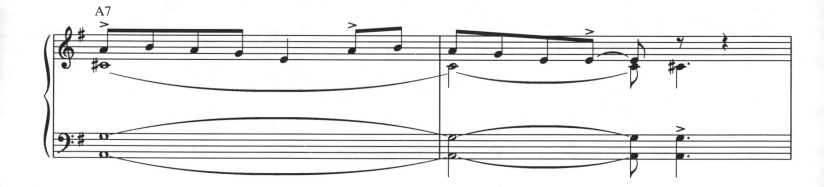

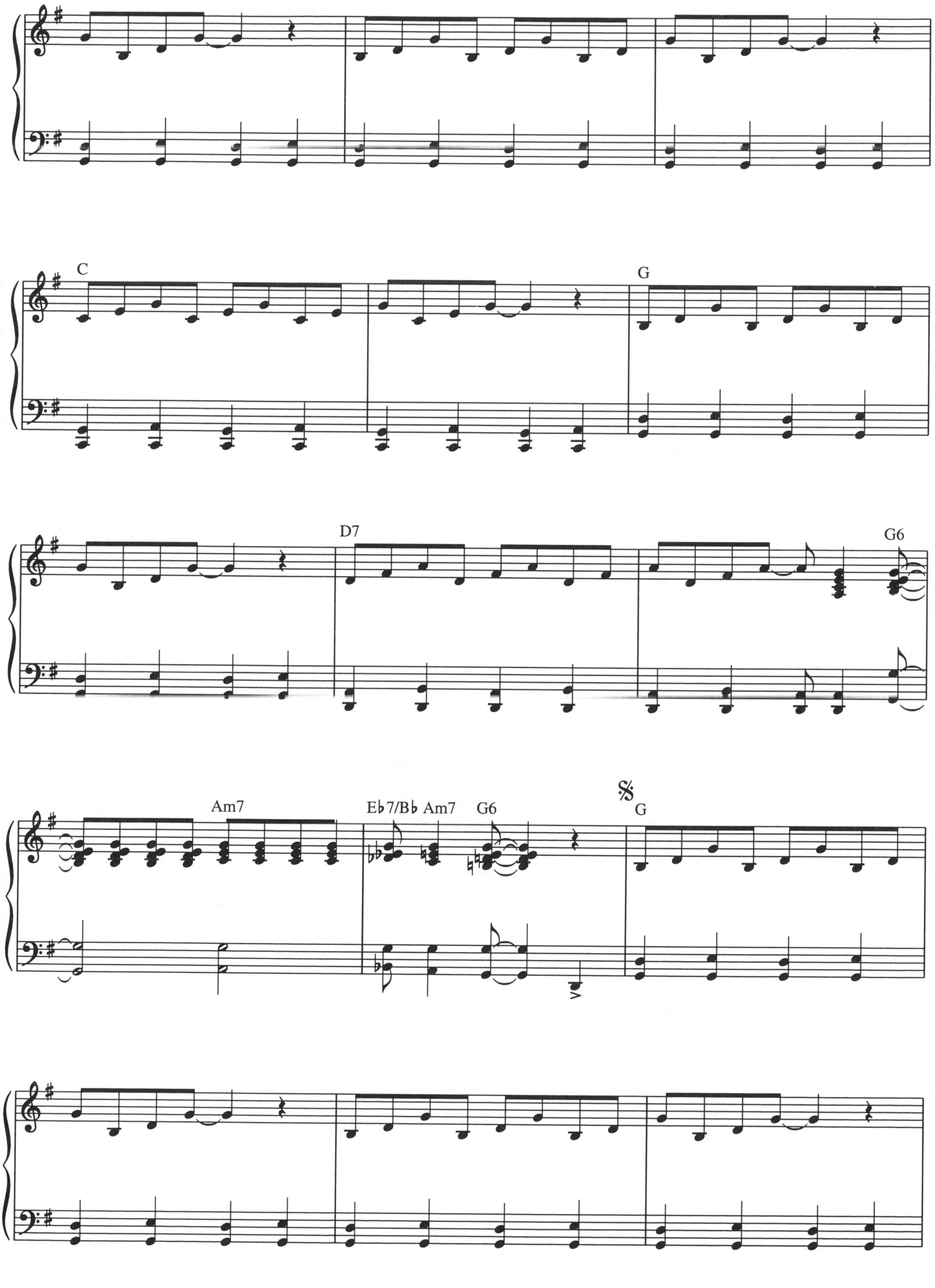
C
G
D7
G6
Am7
E♭7/B♭
Am7
G6
G

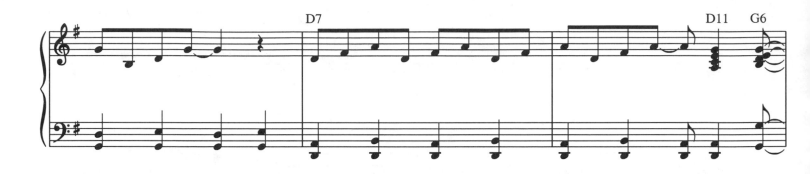
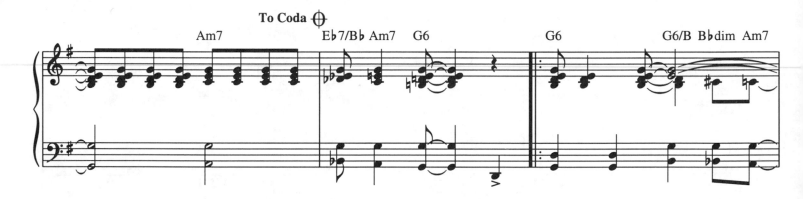

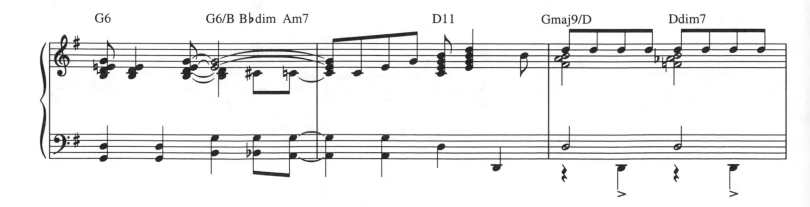

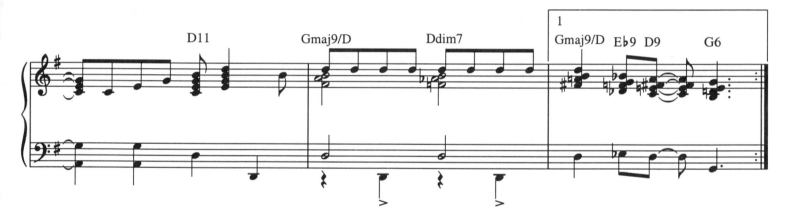

IT ALL DEPENDS ON YOU
from THE SINGING FOOL

Words and Music by B.G. DeSYLVA,
LEW BROWN and RAY HENDERSON

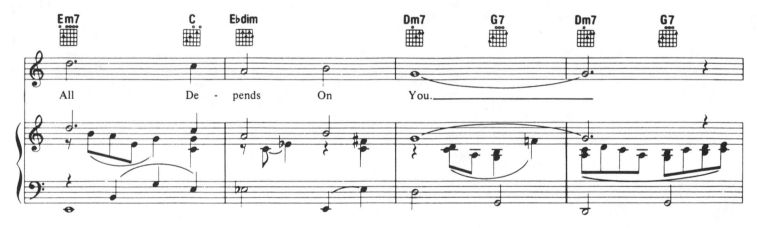

IT WILL HAVE TO DO UNTIL THE REAL THING COMES ALONG

Words and Music by MANN HOLINER, ALBERTA NICHOLS,
SAUL CHAPLIN, L.E. FREEMAN and SAMMY CAHN

104

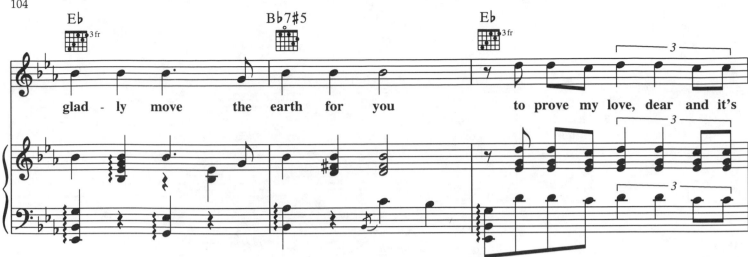

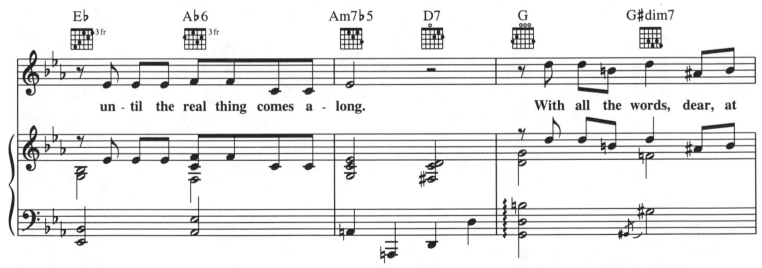

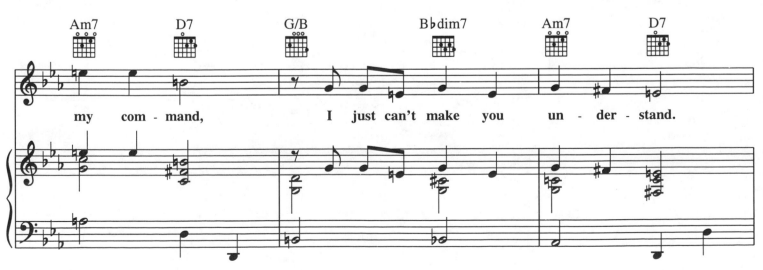

THE JOINT IS JUMPIN'
from AIN'T MISBEHAVIN'

Words by ANDY RAZAF
and J.C. JOHNSON
Music by THOMAS "FATS" WALLER

JUNE NIGHT

Words by CLIFF FRIEND
Music by ABEL BAER

LOOK FOR THE SILVER LINING

from SALLY

Words by BUDDY DeSYLVA
Music by JEROME KERN

Moderately

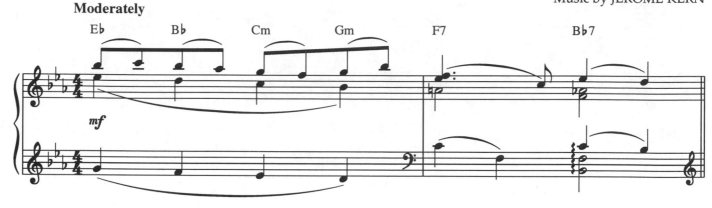

As I wash my dish - es, I'll be fol - low - ing your plan,

Till I see the bright - ness in ev - 'ry pot and pan.

blue. Re - mem - ber some - where

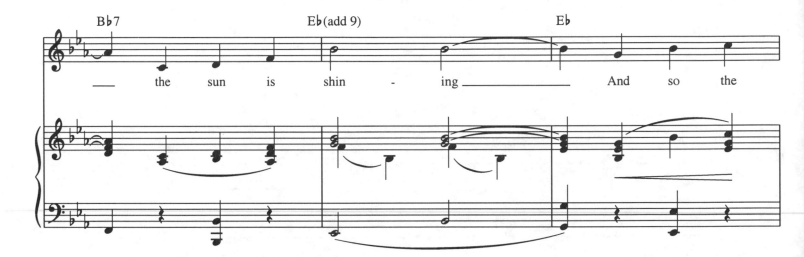

the sun is shin - ing And so the

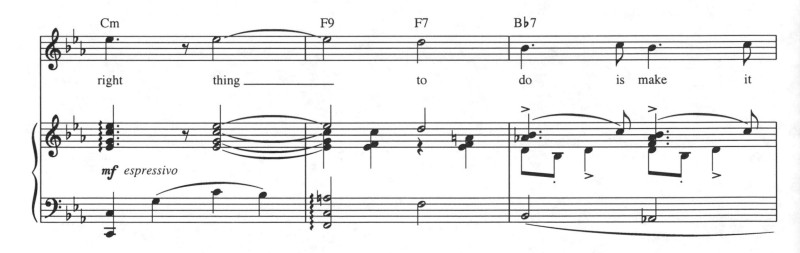

right thing to do is make it

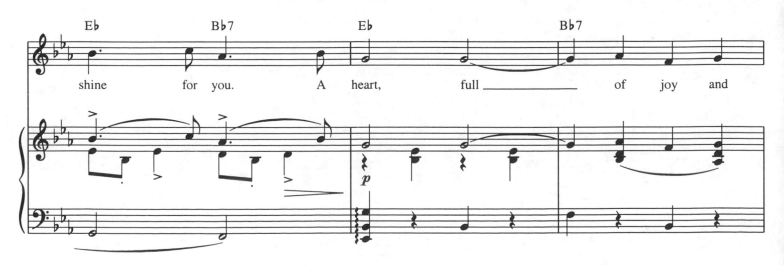

shine for you. A heart, full of joy and

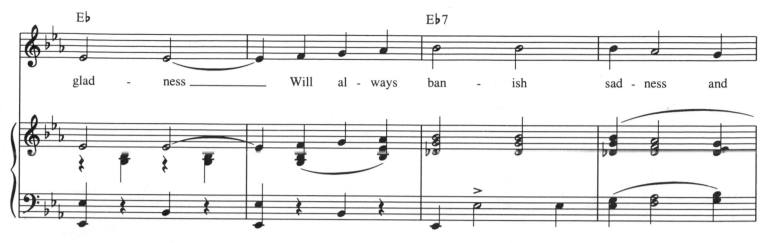

glad - ness _____ Will al - ways ban - ish sad - ness and

strife _____ So al - ways look for _____ the sil - ver

lin - ing _____ And try to find the sun - ny side of

life. life. _____

MARGIE

Words by BENNY DAVIS
Music by CON CONRAD
and J. RUSSELL ROBINSON

Moderately

You can talk a-bout your love af-fairs, _____ Here's one
You can pic-ture me most ev-'ry night, _____ I can't

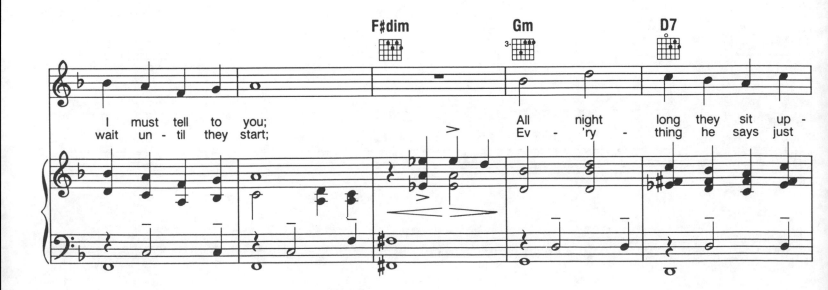

I must tell to you; All night long they sit up-
wait un-til they start; Ev- 'ry- thing he says just

MISSOURI WALTZ
(Hush-A-Bye, Ma Baby)

Words by J.R. SHANNON
Music by JOHN VALENTINE EPPEL

'Way down in Mis - sou - ri where I heard this mel - o - dy,

When I was a lit - tle child___ on my Mom-my's knee; The

old folks were hum - min', Their ban - jos were strum-min' So___

sweet and low.___

Strum, strum, strum, strum, strum, Seems I

hear those ban-jos play - in' once a - gain, Hum, hum,

hum, hum, hum, That same old plain - tive strain.____

Interlude

123

MOOD INDIGO

from SOPHISTICATED LADIES

Words and Music by DUKE ELLINGTON,
IRVING MILLS and ALBANY BIGARD

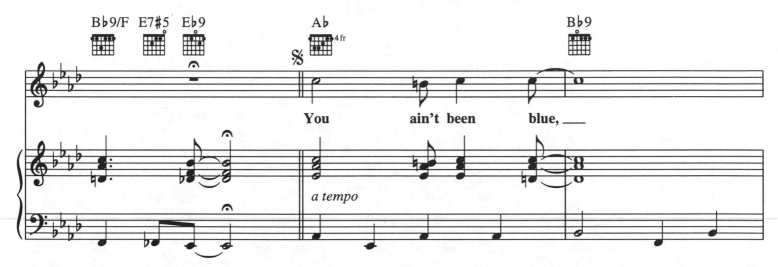

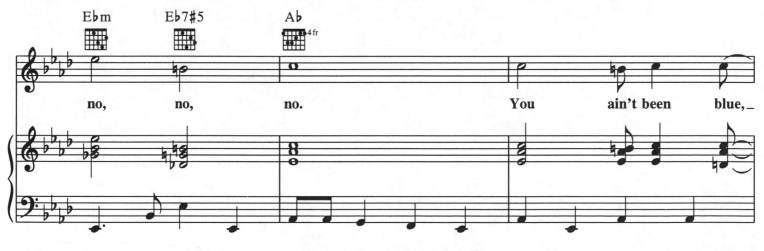

127

SMILES

Words by J. WILL CALLAHAN
Music by LEE S. ROBERTS

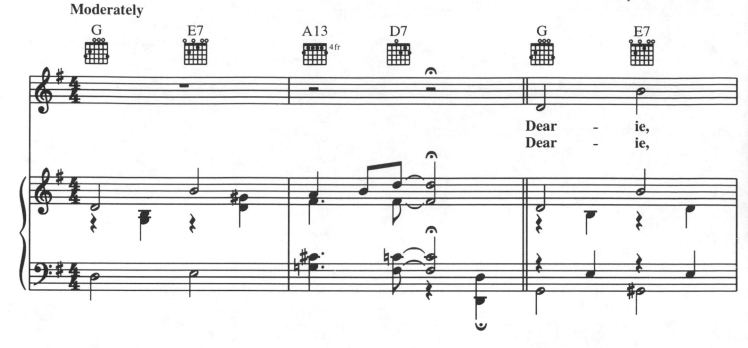

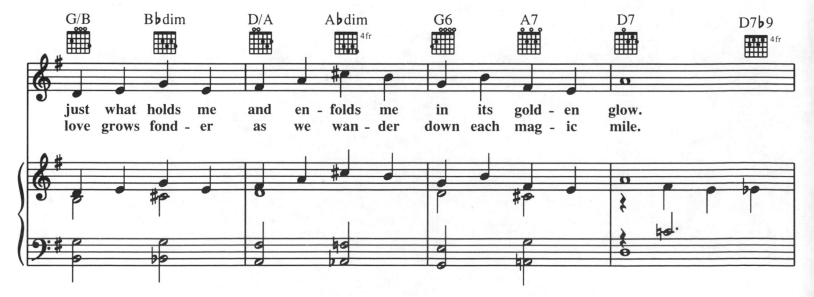

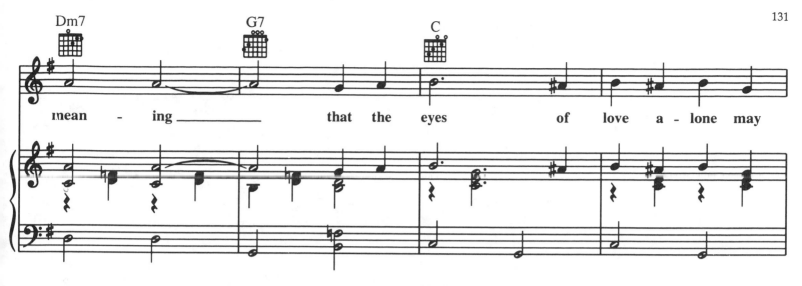

meaning _____ that the eyes of love a - lone may

see, _____ and the smiles that fill my life with

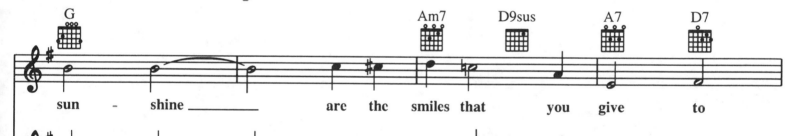

sun - shine _____ are the smiles that you give to

me. There are me. _____

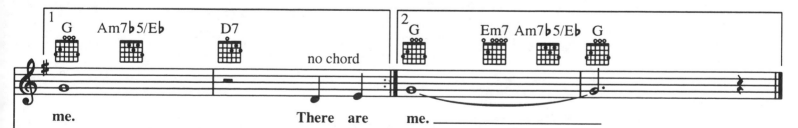

SOMEBODY LOVES ME

from SHE LOVES ME

Words by B.G. DeSYLVA and BALLARD MacDONALD
Music by GEORGE GERSHWIN
French Version by EMELIA RENAUD

Moderately

When this world be-gan it was Heav-en's plan.

There should be a girl for ev-'ry sin-gle man.

To my great re-gret

ST. LOUIS BLUES
from BIRTH OF THE BLUES

Words and Music by
W.C. HANDY

I hate to see ___ de ev' - nin' sun go
Been to de Gyp - sy to get ma for - tune
You ought to see ___ dat stove - pipe brown of

down ___ hate to see ___
tole ___ to de Gyp - sy
mine ___ lak he owns ___

Extra Choruses (optional)

Lawd, a blonde-headed woman makes a good man leave the town,
I said a blonde-headed woman makes a good man leave the town,
But a red-head woman makes a boy slap his papa down.

O ashes to ashes and dust to dust,
I said ashes to ashes and dust to dust,
If my blues don't get you my jazzing must.

WHAT'S NEW?

Words by JOHNNY BURKE
Music by BOB HAGGART

STORMY WEATHER
(Keeps Rainin' All the Time)
from COTTON CLUB PARADE OF 1933

Lyric by TED KOEHLER
Music by HAROLD ARLEN

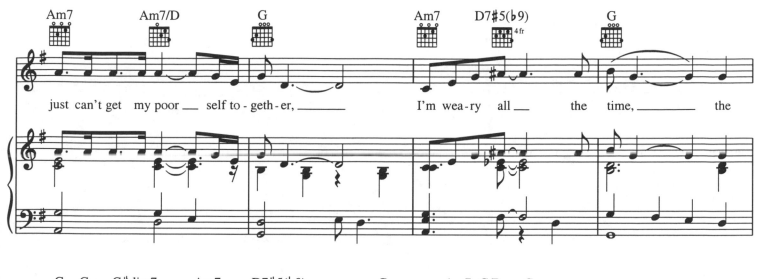

just can't get my poor ___ self to - geth - er, _____ I'm wea-ry all ___ the time, _____ the

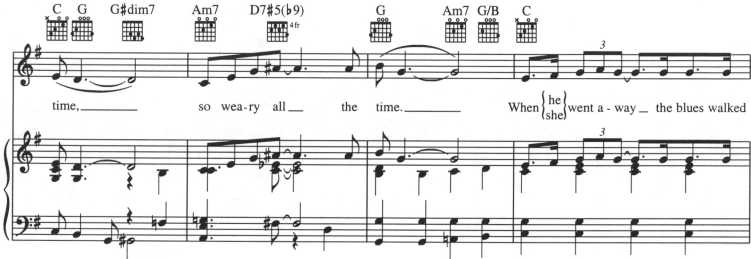

time, _____ so wea - ry all ___ the time. _____ When {he}{she} went a - way ___ the blues walked

in and met me. If {he}{she} stays a - way ___ old rock - in' chair will get me.

All I do is pray ___ the Lord a - bove will let me walk in the sun once more. Can't go on, _____ ev-'ry-thing I had is gone, storm-y

weath - er, _____ since my { man / gal } and I _____ ain't to - geth - er, _____

keeps rain - in' all ____ the time, _____ keeps rain - in' all ____ the

Segue to Interlude | **Fine**

time. _____ time. _____

TOGETHER
from GOOD NEWS

Words and Music by B.G. DeSYLVA,
RAY HENDERSON and LEW BROWN

Moderately Slow

TUXEDO JUNCTION

Words by BUDDY FEYNE
Music by ERSKINE HAWKINS,
WILLIAM JOHNSON and JULIAN DASH

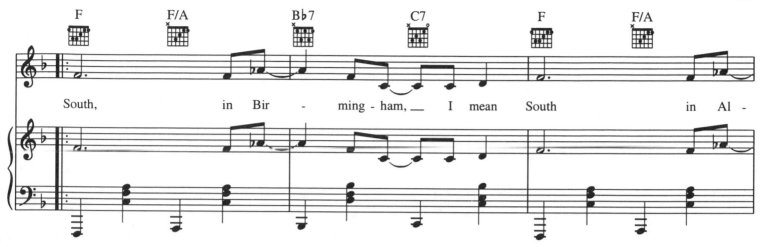

South, in Bir - ming - ham, __ I mean South in Al -

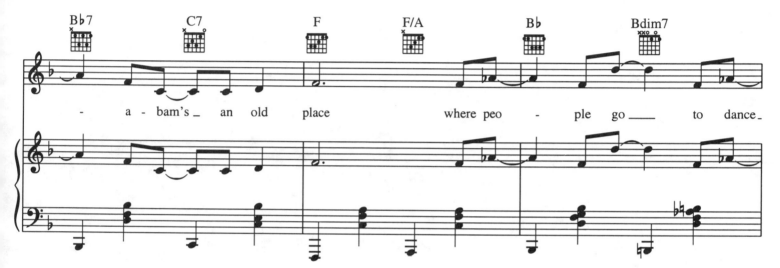

- a - bam's __ an old place where peo - ple go ____ to dance __

____ the night __ a - way. ____ They all drive or walk __

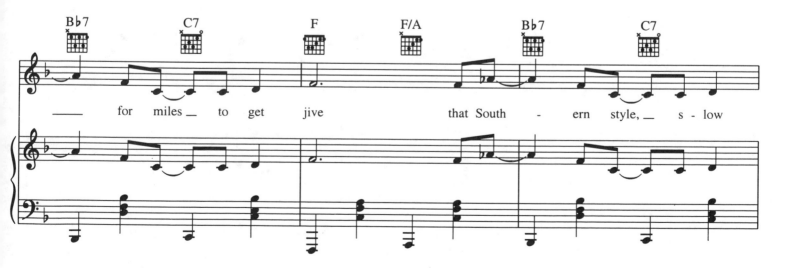

____ for miles __ to get jive that South - ern style, __ s - low

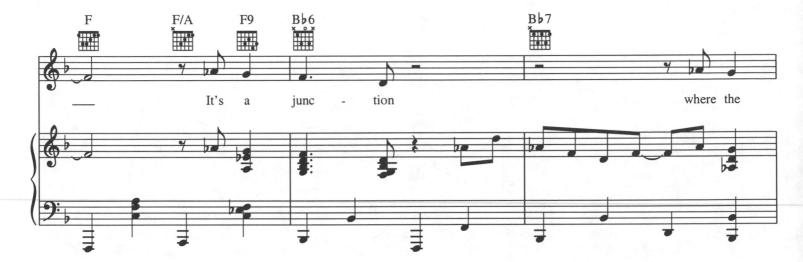

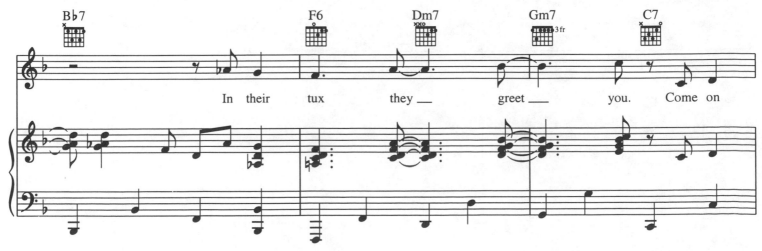

153

down,   for - get _____ your care. _____ Come on

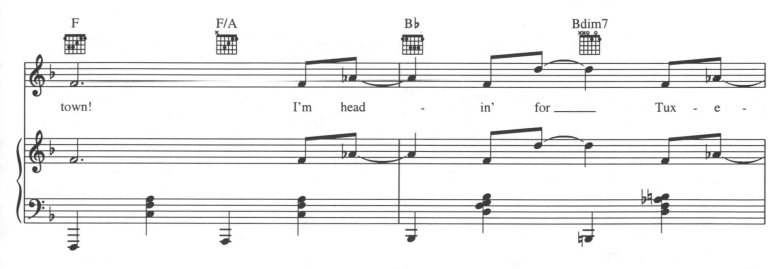

down   you'll find _____ me there. _____ So long

town!   I'm head - in' for _____ Tux - e -

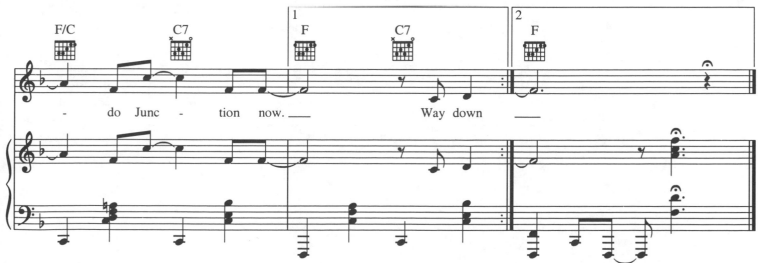

- do Junc - tion now. ___   Way down ___

WHEN I TAKE MY SUGAR TO TEA

from the Paramount Picture MONKEY BUSINESS

Words and Music by SAMMY FAIN,
IRVING KAHAL and PIERRE NORMAN

WHEN YOU'RE SMILING
(The Whole World Smiles with You)

Words and Music by MARK FISHER,
JOE GOODWIN and LARRY SHAY

YOU BETTER GO NOW
from NEW FACES OF 1936

Words by BICKLEY REICHNER
Music by ROBERT GRAHAM

Moderato

Was-n't Mrs.— Pet-ty-bone fun-ny, And is-n't he di-

vine? I un-der-stand he mar-ried her for

YOU'RE MY EVERYTHING

Lyric by MORT DIXON and JOE YOUNG
Music by HARRY WARREN

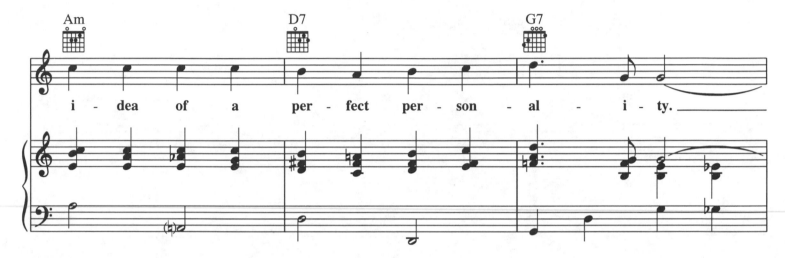

WHO'S SORRY NOW
from THREE LITTLE WORDS

Words by BERT KALMAR
and HARRY RUBY
Music by TED SNYDER